In My Locket

poems

by

Marjorie Moorhead

Finishing Line Press
Georgetown, Kentucky

In My Locket

poems

ACKNOWLEDGMENTS

Grateful acknowledgment goes to the editors of the following journals and
anthologies, in which poems in this book, possibly in earlier versions, first
appeared:

Birchsong: Poetry Centered in VT Vol. II: "All of a Sudden"
Opening Windows Experience/Arts Publishing: "Nettie's Robe"
Sheila Na Gig Online: "Impermanence"
Tiny Seed Literary Poetry of the Wildflowers Anthology: "Now Hear Song"
    (titled here as "Two Months Minus Four Days")
Vermont Historical Society Covid19 Archive: "As the Spring Birds Sing"
Verse-Virtual: "Portrait in My Locket;" "Insomnia Song;" "Solace;"
    "Shrinking it Down to Feathers;" "Let You Go;" "This Year Peonies"
What Rough Beast: "When the Pandemic Is Over"

Also by Marjorie Moorhead
    Survival: Trees, Tides, Song
    Survival Part 2: Trees, Birds, Ocean, Bees
    Every Small Breeze
    What I Ask

My thanks and heart go to Barbara, Nancy, and Martha who together, each
in our own way, helped to ease Dad's last struggles. We formed an unbroken
circle of love.

Publisher: Leah Huete de Maines
Editor: Christen Kincaid
Cover Art and Design: Marjorie Moorhead
Author Photo: Marjorie Moorhead

Order online: www.finishinglinepress.com
        also available on amazon.com

Author inquiries and mail orders:
Finishing Line Press
PO Box 1626
Georgetown, Kentucky 40324
USA

Contents

for Charles

Let us cross over the river and rest under the shade of the trees

—Thomas "Stonewall" Jackson, last words
(a quote Dad liked)

Who can still muddy water and gradually make it clear?

—my tai chi teacher quoting his teacher quoting Lao Tzu,
from *Tao Te Ching* chapter 15

Dad, For the Book

I am using your image as cover for the book.
A photo I took. Back when we were all
relatively unburdened.
It hangs in our hallway, a canvas on the wall.
I'd captured your tenderness, your joy.
You were reading a birthday message.
We surrounded you, to celebrate.
A warm family circle. To honor you.
I am so happy to have the picture
of your smile and a moment
of happiness preserved.
A moment when you knew: you were loved.
You were loved.
I love you.

Portrait In My Locket

I picture him waking for the day,
this retired doctor, father of three,
whose long career was spent caring
for troubled and needy people.
His bed is an island in a room full of boxes.
Stashes of papers, magazines, clothes, books
surround him.
He rises gingerly, and readies for his day
with a wife who tells, on repeat, the same
three stories of her youth, not remembering
she has told them before.
Their little dog, the last remaining of three,
licks him with kisses.

When I Think of You

Love of marmalade
Jelly on an english muffin
A hearty bagel
The loving eyes of a loving sheepdog (Shelby)
or lapdog, even one who has chewed your glasses (Gabby)
A good book (mystery; biography; history)
The Scottish highlands
Green, and White Mountain hikes
A well done cartoon strip
or silly movie (Buster Keaton; Inspector Clouseau)
Bach Cello Suites

The joys of a man with
intelligence, heart, humor
A mensch
My father

Nettie's Robe

It hangs loose and billowy,
colors pushing at the edge of garish;
a strange meeting of delicate and bold.
If not for hook and gravity, it could waft away,
a floral apparition. Silky body-draping fabric,
paisley-like leaves curved and curly,
fabric covered buttons. The sleeve hems have fallen,
robbing them of shape. Intricate floral pattern
conjures subtle whiffs of perfume;
one can almost imagine the bouquet.

Odd this floaty robe is left to remind me
of my paternal grandmother, Nettie.
Short, full figured, she was anything but ephemeral.
As a young child, I sensed strength.
Rock solid opinions rooted in unwavering morality.
A small woman; a large heart.
Firm engulfing hugs established soft security,
promising expansive yet weighty, certain, love.

Her only son, Charles, born in August; a cesarean birth.
Husband Max died young, when Charles was a teen.
How proud she must have been, to see their son become
a father, a doctor. He would live past her,
about forty-five years.

All of a Sudden

Just like that, leaves are red in swaths
tinted by a perennial brush.
Autumn hues orange, gold, yellowed.
All of a sudden, it's cold in morning's hush
and dark. Fog hangs in valleys until the chill has mellowed.

Just like that, sun seems precious.
A limited commodity to be hoarded.
An aid in the battle against scarcity.
All of a sudden, geese fly overhead, squadron sorted,
sailing the clouds toward warmth, squawking commands with levity.

Just like that, I tug for my share of sheet
in morning's chill, instead of pushing it off
to avoid the humid sweat of August.
All of a sudden, t-shirts aren't enough,
long pants are pulled from drawers, thick sweaters become a must.

Just like that my little blond-haired boys look like men.
At the table, my husband and I shadowed with long silence.
Parents seem brittle like branches, dry, and primed to snap.
All of a sudden, life's like a movie, scenes gone by in sequence.
Family pets grown old. I rock them,
our small moments and big events piled in my lap.

What Keeps Me Up

What keeps me up
this late September night?
Is it the Harvest Moon shining

neon through windows,
an incongruous brightness?
Or, is it thoughts that my father

might be dying, slowly, of failing parts
and difficulties,
his wife unable to remember

from one moment to the next, that she's
told that story before. Over and over,
unchanging, but each time apparently fresh

in her mind. And Dad is growing hunched
and shrunken, pain and fatigue
making it onerous to function.

My husband's breaths come loud and regular
as I lay restless beside him, yearning
for merciful surrender into sleep.

Daddy

I want you to know
you are doing an amazing job

holding things together
that are poised to explode

into chaos and disfunction.
You are managing like a hero.

Your wife's Alzheimer's and Crohn's,
your diabetes, high blood pressure,

back pain, and depression.
Your cluttering disorder

and her disabilities are making home
a crazy place.

Quickly becoming unlivable.
Untenable.

But you, dear Father, soldier on
a Warrior of Maintenance.

I hope you feel my love.
I honor you.

Insomnia Song

Sleep, come to me.
I long for your embrace.
To wake in the morning, refreshed,
ready to face the seasons, come what may.

Sleep, come to me.
I'll ride your rolling waves to shore,
lapping sand, rocks, shells,
salty and bleached from the sun.

Sleep, come to me.
Let me float in your clouds'
morphing form,
a white pillowy mist.

Sleep come to me,
and we will see what tolls are paid
to enter a highway of dreams.

Sleep, gentle sleep, I breathe you in,
and out.
I ride you up,
and down.
My pulse has slowed, my frown is gone.
Be my guardian.

Daddy's Girl

Looking like a baby owl
in this picture-framed moment.

Father owl, in horn-rimmed glasses,
smiles knowingly.

The angle at which I lean in,
the tipped neck,

allowing my young-girl head
to lay on his shoulder,

reveals all.
Adoration;

the need for love.
Father-daughter things.

There's a baby-gate in the background,
which shows younger sister had arrived.

I am grabbing a moment,
as the middle child.

Not the first daughter.
Not the new baby.

Just the one in the middle,
craving love.

As the Spring Birds Sing

coronavirus diary XII 4/13/2020

As birds sing of Spring,
we sit in sorrow.
Under pandemic lockdown, not sure
of our tomorrow,
jobs and livelihood disappear.
Hunkered down in required isolation,
each day, we're losing ones held dear;
uncles, teachers, grocery store workers.
Elder parents sealed in their eldercare homes
wave to family through locked doors and windows.
As we shelter within our enclosing walls,
red foxes roam, hedgehogs wander.
Left to usher in Spring without human hustle
and bustle, Earth catches her breath.
We hide behind masks, scramble for ventilators,
as birds build nests in the branches and bramble.
This year, crowded hospitals' beds groan
as Lilac boughs bud, preparing to blossom.

When the Pandemic Is Over

There will be something else.
Pessimistic, I know…
but, will the Planet even be living?
Will it be nurturing home to a species
who've abused and disrespected it so?

When the pandemic ends, I will hug
my father who's been sealed up
into the pod of his elder care home.
I will dance and sing, wave feathers,
light a smudge stick.
I will feel good for my son who's still trying
to have college experience.
And my other son who's been working "remotely".

When the pandemic ends when it ends
Will it end?
Will there be another, different virus?
Will we have killed off all underprivileged
and underserved, leaving only
previously pampered survivors?

When the pandemic ends, I will pick a bouquet
and smell the flowers.
I will drink pure clear water and wade
at the meeting of sand and surf on a beach
where there are only shells and no plastics
strewn or oil surfacing in footprints.

When the pandemic ends
we'll sit around a campfire
and tell our tales. We will remember the lost;
the dead and damaged.

When the pandemic ends, will I have learned
something? Anything?
There will be tv shows, plays and books
about it. We have to tell our stories.

When the pandemic ends
ends
ends.
Fingertips will touch another
and really feel
feel
the surface of a skin
that isn't our own.

When the pandemic ends
clean air will be valued.
Breathing will be sacred.
We will build statues to our lungs.
The shape of lungs, like a heart.

Breath. Breathing.
Feeling. Seeing.
When the pandemic ends.

Breakthrough

When sky's been a sheet of grey,
one solid colorless color, no holes
or cracks for light to beam through,
I settle in, with it tucked up in my heart.
Familiar vague listlessness, waves
of unmoored thoughts, I'm waiting
for blue to break through.
And then, walking in snow that mirrors
this sky, I see small cones, dropped from high
pines. Bucketfuls have been scattered
like chicken feed in a barnyard.
Alongside, small tracks pressed into the winter white.
Dotted lines forming many trails, each a story-map
of journey in the night. Reminders I'm not alone
here in a sea of pale, endless cloud. Unseen, wind blows
singing through green pine boughs, small furred beings
scurry, and we all wait together for the blue skies
that come. Eventually they come and we bask in warmth
as the opening occurs, letting sun rush in like a river
fed by streams that had dried but now swell to brim
fresh with rain, relieving pain and longing,
restoring depleted reservoirs with life sustaining quench.

Perfect Distraction

When the cardinal sings,
into a white-clouded morning,
outside our bathroom window
at the perfect height to reach me,
he on upper branches of the apple tree,
me on our second floor,
we're face-to-face.

Clear and insistent tune, wed to glorious
red, the perfect distraction.
Pulls me away from looping thoughts
of leg pain, taxes due, aging parents,
aging spouse, nearly independent children
morphing warp-speed. Over-dusty house,
virus killing so many, structural, bricked-into-system
inequality. War-grade weapons in off-kilter hands;
addled brains, soaked in conspiracy theory lies,
mowing down scapegoated innocents like flies.

Instead, just tree, sky behind,
the song of a bird
who means business, saying,
pay attention; listen, and see.
Yes. Yes, I will let this moment
hold me, fill me.

Solace

Snubbed by it, I understand the value of sleep
so well just now.

The velvety comfort of it. Waking refreshed, clear,
renewed. *You don't know what you've got til*

it's gone. Yes, indeed, Joni Mitchell. You called it,
and so young.

I will go to music, whenever possible, for solace.
Wrap it around me like a quilt,

relax into the warmth. Let a good ballad grab hold
and melt like campfire marshmallows sliding

down their stick. A voice skewered with aching
lyrics over a jangly bare-boned tune stabs

the target every time, and takes me away
to a place I can rest.

There, I'll sit in the lap of well-sung struggle,
ache, emotion, longing,

let it all bleed out,
and lay my burden down.

Hold My Father

> *"I buried my father/ in the sky./ Since then, the birds/ clean and comb him every morning/ and pull the blanket up to his chin/ every night."* *

I hold my father in the sky
in the clouds
in my heart

as he lies
restlessly on a hospital bed
with so many cords attached

to his skin, connecting
heart, lungs, *life*
to monitors.

I send him the comfort
of a breeze blowing through,
cooling on a hot day,

the sound of birds, giving
his soul what it needs
to find serenity.

*excerpt from "Little Father" from *Book of My Nights* Copyright 2001 by Li-Young Lee. Reprinted with the permission of The Permissions Company, LLC on behalf of BOA Editions, Ltd., *boaeditions.org*

Comfort and Pleasure

As I have walked early,
into the morning light beaming
through new tree blossoms
dressing the trees as if for a wedding,
presenting the bride as a budding,
open, fragrant gift to the world,
and have let my thoughts wander
free, to the beat of my heart
and the rhythm of my breath,
I am ready to receive the rest
of this day
in which my father lies in a hospital
bed, hooked up to IV diuretics, and monitors
of this and that, and my children are about
to hit the road, traveling through
states to come here, their childhood home,
in our car, now overdue for inspection.
I cough and sneeze and blow blow blow
the irritating pollen out of my body
as my husband in next room practices
qui gong exercises, following a video
on the desk top computer screen. He is
convalescing while trying to get his knee,
shoulder, chest, and arm muscles to cooperate,
and we both secretly wonder if he will ever
be getting back to the physically demanding work
he's always done.
The birds know it is Spring and relentlessly sing,
and sing their varied songs. They fly
from branch to branch, so busy in the business
of feeding, nesting, chirp, and tweeting.
I'll seek comfort and take pleasure observing their meeting.

Tree, Be My Arms

Today, I let branches speak
for my heart and I let them
calm my mind as I depend
on the gentleness of apple blossoms
just blooming on our tree.
Light pink, barely a shade above
white, and the lime green of newness
draping each arm in ceremony.
Celebration of what is,
what might come to be,
and what will surely pass.

I hold you, dear father,
in this particular beauty;
the comfort it can bring,
and ask that you rest
in something like acceptance and love.
Hoping to see you tomorrow.
May it be in gentle serenity,
rather than sorrow.

It's Morning and My Father Still Lives

My sisters sit with him, keeping watch.
I wait for their report and tussle with the thought
of driving back over to the new and luxurious hospice
center where he lies.

There, he lies in a bed, almost all machines gone now
except the drip of medicine into one arm,
which keeps him from experiencing a suffocation
feeling, when his very weak heart can't quite
get enough oxygen pumping through his blood.
The other arm gets another drug, which keeps
his anxiety in check. Amazing. Can that truly work?

Dad can't tell us anymore. He lies, slack mouthed
with the green oxygen tubing at his nostrils.
When he needs adjusting in the bed, it takes two nurses
to get him all set. Back when he could, he told us that this is OK.
He made the switch from keeping-alive-by-all-means
to "comfort care". And we are so grateful to all be on the same page.
The human body dies. It does not travel on forever;
the machine breaks down, either part by part or
in a massive rebellion of sudden failure.

Our Dad has been a warrior of lasting and enduring
but now, it is time to ease away.
May it be ease. May he not struggle or worry.
May he feel love and serenity. We will now be the carriers
of his beautiful story.
It is written in my heart.

This Year Peonies

I'm viewing the Peonies
differently this year.
Almost hostile; in-your-face
too fancy for their own good.
Almost nasty, those garish ruffles
blaring pink, or white; too many petals
all flouncing out at once
like dancing petticoats.
No sense of reserve or making space
for others. No holding back, giving room
to feelings which may be tender, delicate,
in need of quiet and a solemn realm
in which to process sorrow,
maybe wallow a bit in the harsh aftermath
of a loved one's drawn out demise.
The hard fought journey a struggle
full of trials and tribulations.
And now is a time for stepping lightly;
for wrapping the quilt up close,
seeking quietude and solace.
Shoring up for those arrows of piercing pain
that come sailing when missing,
and the finality of loss sink in.
Peonies, I'll pass you by
and not linger in the scent.
Not this year
when your beauty is a bit more
than I can bear.

When His Soap Runs Out My Heart Will Break

Dad's Dial soap. It foams. A lovely apple green,
a subtle scent. Anti-bacterial, of course.
My father with the surgically clean hands.
Never a hint of dirt under any fingernails.
Beautiful hands on a beautiful man.
In the end, a stiffly arched finger unable to lengthen
making it hard to manage cuff buttons at his wrists.

Toward the end, which lasted a fair while,
I did his pharmacy shopping. While drilling
drug names and his birth year into my memory,
this also intimated which drinks and snacks he favored
(Pepsi - the "real sugar" kind; Cranberry Juice Cocktail,
pretzels), and his preferred hand soap.

Dad has been gone over a month; not yet two.
We emptied his place. There were items to choose.
I kept a reading chair, books, jigsaw puzzles,
his smooth walking stick, some photographs,
two ribbed cotton undershirts that held his scent
—how long will that last? along with
his foaming soap to use.

Two Months Minus Four Days

Walking solo as weed feelings grow,
scraggly; wild in the verges.
Seeking solace. Wanting rain. A soothing
soak turns from bones to feathers the burden
of mourning.
Spiky and smooth, a field of fringed leaves
sparkles. Now sing the colors
of thistle, vetch, and clover.
Sing the yellows and purples
of your bruises; the deep burgundy
of your heart, the blue
veins of each scar.
Honor your father's fears and favorites
with this wild wandering. Remember
the Teton trails; switchback zigzagging,
wildflower swaths and the strong calves,
muscle furred in hairs above wool socks
and sturdy laced boots.
This was his pleasure realized. Steep in it;
hear the whistling song.

From Clouds to Winter

Clouds, like fur of a calico cat,
sit in delineated puffs, foregrounding
powder blue sky.
Still green-leafed trees cover rolling hillsides below.
It is September. I've walked in a beautiful day,
and am now craving chocolate.
The beauty outside my window is astounding
yet...apprehension colors corners of floating thoughts,
like glorious goldenrod becoming browned and brittle,
up on the hill. Anxiety seeped in the slant of afternoon sun.
Earlier darkness in evenings. Closed windows at night.
Geese flying overhead. All markers
of hovering
Winter.

Shrinking it Down to Feathers

I went for a walk, and there
were the clouds. Finessed on the sky,
like paint layered on canvas. Stroked
in soft colors; calm; beautiful. Grey, white,
like the feathers on some graceful bird.
It was quiet; just one crow, a lone plane.
The trees half turned toward Autumn;
some leaves colored, some fallen.

Near the library, I see a friend out walking with her dog.
We exchange stories of hardship. Her grandson, back to hospital
for stem cell grafts. My parents, one gone in June;
we'll be spreading his ashes on a mountain top soon. The other,
my Mother, had taken a fall, causing great fear.

As her dog settles down from excited greetings to cuddles,
Linda and I consider how to cope…with stress, with worries,
with sadness.
At times, I say, *it all shrinks down to noticing the clouds,
and carrying that with you.* Linda agrees. Solace in small
daily moments of beauty is what we grasp; how we endure.

Not asking for more. Finding amazement in less.
Letting that be a place of rest, of hope.
Color of sky, shape of leaf, wind on skin,
small steady blessings.

On the way home, I make sure
to walk past the river, and check for geese.

Impermanence

When the surf soaks the sand,
water spreads like a bedsheet being

wafted over and onto its mattress.
Hovering, then receding, back into the source,

leaving a shadow of itself,
sinking, and disappearing,

a ghost of the wave.
Water recasts into sand, wet becomes

not-wet in a shimmering moment,
sometimes revealing strands of seaweed

and bits of shell left behind, escaping
a pull back into the sea.

Footprints become melted shapes
of themselves. Erased forever,

mixed again into the same
grains that formed them.

Signs

I wake looking for birds.
I waken as they come faithfully
to black oil sunflower seeds offered
at our deck. A path from tree to seeds
welcomes their feathered bodies,
allowing me to sink into the soft
tomato red or wear the black mask
or flit the blue tail or lift bright tufted head.
Resting in their flight and feeding,
I am nourished for my day
of two legged walking, dogged plodding,
trying for acceptance of come-what-may.

I'll wait for the fog to rise, tree tops emerging.
I'll hope for the sun to highlight
any determined leaves remaining
and also those that surrendered and now surround
my footsteps on sidewalks layered with acorns,
maple seed pods, berries and nuts I can't name.
A trail-mix whose ingredients are signs of the season.
Last blast bright colors that tell a tale of pale to come.
Time of prescribed patience and quietude in grey and blue.
An interlude one must learn to endure by embracing
retreat, and letting feathers come to view.

Now (Dad)

Now   you won't see the red leaves
         or, do you?

Now   you won't feel the cold winds
         chill in the air the frost
         of mornings. Mourning.

Now   when I think of you it's free of worry
         but full of ache
         knowing I'll never hear the warm voice
         the chuckle at a known joke
         winked at between us.

         All the understanding you gave
         is carried in my body
now.
         to remain strong, or fade with memory.
         Which?

How   long can I conjure you
         in true essence?
         I still see the smile; the teeth.
         I still feel the heart; its kindness.
         And you; your spirit… are you
         at rest?

How   I love you
         miss you
         grasp on to the knowing of you
         feel a chasm your leaving has left.

Now   I must wear you on my heart
         like a sweater vest,
         a Scottish tam, a Kangol cap.

Hugging Him

Where has my father gone
after almost one year passing

Where has my father gone
now he's not here with us anymore

He's missed the growing of grandchildren
He's missed the latest war

Maybe he's somewhere kinder,
not rife with destruction and gloom

Maybe it's glittery tinsel there,
shining silver, like the moon

Maybe he's with the old dogs now,
beloved years ago

Maybe they walk in Scotland,
bagpipes soundtracking steady strides

Mountains and lakes surround them there
Hearty ale awaits at the pub

Maybe Charles is relaxing in fresh, cool air
Around him, Cello Suites float a gentle tide

Bach's notes holding, soothing,
hugging him tenderly, tight.

Let You Go

I place my father gently
in the blue chair that remains.
Blue fabric, wooden frame.
It rocks, and reclines.
My husband sits there now.
He may have found a dog's hair,
holds it up for my inspection.
Sun beams in, blankets the chair with warmth.
There, where man and dog sat, companions.

My father's light went off. He was here;
now, he's not. There was a moment
when he ended. And, is now no more.
Except for memory. How long will that last?
How strong?

Gently, I place my father in his chair
reconstructing the round head,
the bearded jaw. His dress, *tweed*. His scent,
slightly sweet. His laugh, *a chuckle*. Stay with me
Dad. Don't fade away.
Stay in the chair, relax awhile. I don't want
to let you go.

In a Dream, You Say Yes

Dad, last night you came in a dream
to say, *Yes*, it's OK to make a book of the poems
I wrote, those days when you were leaving us,
and in the shadows of loss when you'd gone.

You were not quite you, in the dream—it was
a man with your shape head and your white beard,
and he was smiling at me, and then—it was your smile,
it was you.

I didn't remember this until later, after
having tossed and turned all night,
getting up and going down, a restlessness
in the legs that I know we shared.

Thank you, Dad, for your blessing here,
that gentle smile and sparkle the permission I've needed,
to tip over my bucket of grief, letting free a flow of
tender memory, and flowering blossoms of loving legacy.

Marjorie Moorhead writes from a river valley, surrounded by mountains and four season change, at the border of NH/VT. She found a voice in poetry after surviving AIDS in its early years, and becoming a mother. Much of her work addresses survival, environment, relationship, and appreciation of the everyday. She is author of *Every Small Breeze* (Kelsay Books 2023), *What I Ask* (Kelsay 2024), the chapbooks *Survival: Trees, Tides, Song* (Finishing Line Press, 2019) and *Survival Part 2: Trees, Birds, Ocean, Bees* (Duck Lake Books, 2020). Her poems have appeared in journals including *Amethyst Review, Tiny Seed Literary, Moist Poetry Journal, Bloodroot Literary, Sheila-Na-Gig, Porter House Review, Poeming Pigeon, Verse-Virtual, What Rough Beast, A River Sings, The Poet's Touchstone*, and others. Her poems are found in a large number of anthologies, including those that benefit environmental, women's, Covid first responder, and refugee aid organizations. Marjorie's local poetry group is 4th Friday Poets, a small group that has been meeting twice a month for years. In summer of 2019 Marjorie enjoyed participating in a workshop at Fine Arts Work Center, Provincetown MA, thanks to a tuition scholarship from Indolent Books. She has attended many readings and workshops online with some amazing and inspiring poets, thanks to zoom. Along with poetry community, love of family, daily walks in each season, and tai chi practice are the things that feed her.

www.ingramcontent.com/pod-product-compliance
Lightning Source LLC
Chambersburg PA
CBHW022052080426
42734CB00009B/1309